The Storm

The Storm

STORIES & PROSE POEMS

BY

KAHLIL GIBRAN

TRANSLATED BY JOHN WALBRIDGE

WHITE CLOUD PRESS
SANTA CRUZ, CA

FIRST EDITION

Cover Illustration by Kahlil Gibran, Gift of Mrs. Mary Haskell Minis
Courtesy, Museum of Fine Arts, Boston
Cover Design by Daniel Cook
Printed in the United States of America

Library of Congress Cataloging in Publication Data
Gibran, Kahlil, 1883-1931
      [Selections. English. 1991]
      The Storm: Stories and Prose Poems / by Kahlil Gibran;
translated by John Walbridge.
          p.   cm.
      ISBN 1-883991-01-3 : $18.00
      I. Title
   PJ7826.I2A277   1993
   892'.735--dc20   93-29510
                                            CIP

Illustration credits
All illustrations by Kahlil Gibran
Crossed Open Embrace, p. 4; Study of a Face, p. 12; Dying Man and
Vulture, p. 44; Untitled drawing, p. 48; Head of Orpheus Floating Down
the River Hebrus to the Sea, p. 52; Untitled watercolor and pencil, p. 82;
Untitled nudes, p. 72; The Heavenly Mother, p. 114; Self-portrait, back
cover, Gifts of Mrs. Mary Haskell Minis, in the collection of Telfair
Academy of Arts and Sciences, Savannah, Georgia. Nude figures
pointing, p. 86, Gift of Mrs. Mary Haskell Minis, Courtesy of Museum
of Fine Arts, Boston.

CONTENTS

Translator's dedication

To Juan, ruh ameen.

Note on Texts

The pieces translated in this collection are taken from Mikhail Naimy, ed., *Al-majmu'a al-kalimah li-mu'allafat Jibran Khalil Jibran*, Beirut, 1961, and were originally published in various Arabic journals and newspapers. They are: "Al-nafs," p. 247; "'Asifa," pp. 427-438; "Al-sha'ira," pp. 477-478; "Ru'ya," pp. 250-251; "Al-'ubudiya," pp. 362-364; "Fi madinat al-amwat," pp. 241-242; "Ya khalili al-faqir," pp. 272-273; Surakh al-qubur," pp. 96-105; "Bayna layl wa-sabh," pp. 389-393; "Manaha fi'l-haql," pp. 273-274; "Al-wahda wa'l-infirad," pp. 560-563; "Safina fi dubab," pp. 493-502; "Al-quwa al-'amya'," pp. 296-297; and "Amama 'arsh al-jamal," pp. 265-266.

Introduction

Kahlil Gibran was born in Bisharri, a Maronite Christian village in the mountains of northern Lebanon, in 1883. His mother was from a family of priests; his father was a minor agent of the local warlord. His childhood was spent in desperate poverty in this place of great beauty. A family friend taught the young Kahlil how to read. When he was 12, his mother attempted to escape her troubles by emigrating to the United States with her children. From the ethereal beauty of the Lebanese mountains, Kahlil found himself amidst the squalor of the Boston slums. His mother scraped out a meager living for herself and her children as a peddler.

The young Kahlil's lovely drawings attracted the attention of a social worker, who put him in touch with Fred Holland Day, an avant-garde photographer and publisher, who used Gibran and his family as models and introduced Gibran to the literary world of 1890s Boston. His new friends, charmed by this talented Lebanese boy, introduced him to modern art, gave him books to read by such authors as Nietzsche, and took him to plays and concerts. Thus, although his education in America was very uneven—he never really learned to spell, for example, and was always more comfortable writing in Arabic—he became accustomed to traveling in literary circles while still a teenager. He still lived with his family amidst the poverty of the Syrian ghetto in Boston's South End.

In 1896, he returned to Lebanon for high school, where he acquired the rudiments of an Arabic literary education. Soon after he returned to America and his intellectual friends in 1902, his mother, sister, and half-brother died, leaving him alone in America with his surviving sister. During the next few years he began working seriously as an artist and attracted somewhat wider attention, even exhibiting in a small way. He also began to write for the Arabic newspapers published in America. His prose poems, simple parables written without the rhetorical elaborations of traditional Arabic poetry, quickly made him a major figure among Arabic writers in America. In 1908 one of his American friends, Mary Haskell, supplied the funds for him to go to Paris to study art.

Returning to America in 1910, he worked continuously on his drawings and paintings and continued to write for the Arabic newspapers. In 1912 he moved to New York to be closer to the centers of art and Arabic literature in America. His art earned him only a precarious living, and he was forced to depend on the assistance of friends, particularly Mary Haskell, a talented and independent woman who was the headmistress of a girls' school in Boston. When Gibran began writing seriously in English, she served as his editor; the form of his English writings owes much to her assistance and judgment. His first English work was *The Wanderer*, a collection of prose poems and parables. By this time he was well established as a major modern Arabic writer. *The Prophet*, his best known work, was written over a number of years and finally published in 1923. This and the other English works that followed it eventually gave Gibran a degree of financial independence. He continued to work on his paintings, but his health began to deteriorate. He died on April 10, 1931. Despite the objections of the church authorities, who had been offended by his anti-clerical writings, he received a religious funeral. At his instructions, his body was taken back to be buried in his home village of Bisharri and the royalties of his book's were divided between his sister, the only surviving member of his immediate family, and his village.

Gibran is first of all an Arabic writer. Arabic was his native language and the language he was always most comfortable with. Even after living in America for most of his life, he would still write a poem first in Arabic and then translate it into English. His Arabic works are remarkable, free of the exaggerated rhetoric and strict traditional forms characteristic of Arabic poetry up to his time. His simple diction and new forms revolutionized Arabic literature. Except for a short novel, *Broken Wings,* a verse dialogue, *Processions,* and some one act plays, all of his Arabic writings were in the form of short pieces—stories, parables, and prose poems—written for newspapers and magazines. Many were later collected and published as collections.

The themes of his Arabic works are those familiar to readers of his English works: nature against society, spirituality, natural beauty, human injustice, and the destruction of the spirit by society. Most of his Arabic works were written before his books in English. They are more passionate and fresh, on the whole, than the English work, being products of his youth. The influences that shaped his writing were obvious. Most important was the contrast between the beauty of his native Lebanese mountains and the squalor of Boston and New York, where he lived most of his life. Lebanon, romanticized by exile, is the real setting of all his works. He championed the freedom and simplicity of the individual against the rigidities of society and protested the oppression of the weak, the poor, and women. He denounced the hypocrisy of organized religion, particularly his own Maronite church. Though his romanticism and anarchism may seem naive, the intensity of his feelings, the energy of his ideas, and the universality of the disquiet which he voices speak to modern men and women.

Gibran's Arabic writings were translated after his death. These translations are not particularly good. Most are more or less inelegant and some are extremely inaccurate and misleading. Gibran's reputation has suffered from them. We undertook the present series to provide fresh, contemporary, and accurate translations of Gibran's significant Arabic work. The translations follow the original as closely as practical without doing violence to English style. We have not tried to imitate Gibran's English style since we think that his Arabic works deserve to be judged on their own considerable merits.

The texts in this volume are a selection of pieces on related themes drawn from various periods of Gibran's life, the earliest written soon after his return from art school in Paris and the last in the years just before the publication of *The Prophet*. They reflect several characteristic Gibran themes: the injustice perpetrated by society against the poor, the weak, and the sincere; nature and its destruction by man; and the purity and innocence of young love and its perversion and destruction by society. These prose poems are often angry or bitter or disappointed, although these emotions are balanced by an exultation in the natural. They are quite lacking in the aloof cynicism of much modern literature.

In the absence of a critical edition, we have followed the text of the collected edition of his Arabic works published by his friend Mikhail Naimy.

John Walbridge
New York City
August 1993

The first great moment that I remember was when I was three years old—a storm—I tore my clothes and ran out in it—and I have been doing that in storms ever since. . . .

Kahlil Gibran

The Soul

The Great God separated a soul from His own essence and fashioned beauty within her.

He gave her the mildness of the evening breezes, the fragrance of wildflowers, the gentleness of moonlight.

He gave her a cup of happiness and said, "Drink of it only if you forget the past and are heedless of the future."

He gave her a cup of sorrow and said, "Drink of it and apprehend the essence of life's joy."

He scattered within her a love that will desert her at the first sigh of fulfillment and a sweetness that will desert her at the first word of pride.

From heaven He sent down knowledge upon her to guide her on the paths of truth.

Deep within her He placed discernment to see what cannot be seen.

In her He created a yearning that flows with dreams and runs with spirits.

He clothed her with a robe of longing, woven by angels from rainbow threads.

Then He placed within her the darkness of bewilderment—the image of the light.

Then the Great God took fire from anger's forge and a wind from the desert of ignorance, sand from the shores of the sea of arrogance and dust from the footprints of the ages. With these he molded man.

He gave him a blind power that blazes up in madness and is damped by lusts.

He placed life in him, which is the image of death.

The Great God smiled and wept, looked with love boundless and eternal, and wedded man and his soul.

The Storm

In the thirtieth year of his life Yusof el-Fakhri abandoned the world and all that is in it to live as a silent, ascetic hermit in that solitary cell at the edge of the Qadisha Valley on the north side of Mount Lebanon.

The people of the neighboring villages disagreed about who he was. Some said that he came from a wealthy and distinguished family, but that he had been spurned by the woman he loved. For this reason he had abandoned his old home, seeking solace in solitude. Others said that he was a dreamy poet who had fled from the clamor of society in order to set down his thoughts and sentiments in verse. Others said that he was a pious mystic who was content with his faith and cared nothing for the world. Still others said simply, "He is mad."

I myself held none of these opinions, for I knew that spirits contain dark mysteries that can never be uncovered by idle speculation. I wished to meet this strange man and was eager to converse with him. Twice I sought to approach him in order to find an explanation of what he really was. He only glared and dismissed me rudely with a few chilly words. The first time I encountered him, he was walking near the Cedars. I greeted him as politely as I was able. He returned the greeting with a curt nod, turned, and hurried away from me. The second time I found him standing in the middle of a little vineyard near his cell. I went up to him and said, "Yesterday I heard that a Syrian monk built this cell in the fourteenth century. Do you know anything about that, sir?"

He answered me with a glare: "I do not know who built this hut, nor do I care to know." Then he turned his back on me and added scornfully, "Why don't you ask your grandmother? She is older and knows more about the history of these valleys." So I left him, abashed and ashamed of my childishness.

Two years passed. The life of this enigmatic man enticed my imagination and filled my thoughts and dreams.

II

One day in spring I was wandering among the hills near the cell of Yusof el-Fakhri and was surprised by a storm. Its winds and rain made a plaything of me as the raging sea plays with a ship, waves smashing its rudder and wind rending its sails. I turned toward the cell, saying to myself, "This is a suitable occasion to visit this ascetic, for the storm will be my excuse and sodden clothes my advocate."

I reached the cell in a pitiable state. No sooner did I knock than the man I had so long desired to meet was before me. He held a bird, its head bruised and its feathers crushed, trembling as though it were on the verge of its last breath. After greeting him, I said, "Excuse me, sir, for coming to you in this way, but the storm is violent and I am far from home."

He studied my face and then spoke in a voice tainted with disgust, "There are many caves in this district. You might have taken refuge in one of them."

He said this while stroking the head of the bird with a tenderness the like of which I had never seen in my life. I was astonished by the two opposites—kindliness and severity in a single instant—and I did not know what to do. It was as though he knew what was in my mind. He looked at me, seeking an explanation, and said, "The storm will not eat spoiled meat. Why should you fear it and flee?"

I replied, "The storm may not like meat, spoiled or fresh, but it craves that which is cold and wet. Doubtless it will find me a delicious morsel should it seize me once more."

His face relaxed a little. "Were the storm to consume you, you would attain an honor you are unworthy of."

I replied, "Yes, but sir, I have come to you fleeing the storm so as not to receive that honor which I do not merit!"

He turned his head, trying to conceal a slight smile, and pointed to a wooden bench near a hearth where a fire burned. "Sit and dry your clothes."

Gratefully, I sat down near the fire. He sat opposite me on a bench hewn from the stone. He began dipping the tips of his fingers into an oily mixture in an earthenware cup, rubbing it onto the bird's wings and wounded head. Then he turned to me and said, "The wind seized this thrush and threw it against the rock, leaving it half dead."

I answered, "The wind, sir, also carried me to your door, and now I know not whether it has broken my wing or wounded my head."

He looked at my face with something near concern. "How wonderful it would be if men had the nature of birds, so that the wind could break their wings and crush their heads. But man is by nature fearful and cowardly. No sooner is he roused by the storm than he flees, trying to hide himself among the rocks and caves of the earth."

Pursuing this thought, I said, "Yes, the bird has a nobility that man has not, for man lives in the shadows of laws and customs that he has devised for himself, but the birds live in accordance with the universal and absolute laws that drive the earth around the sun."

His eyes gleamed and his face showed the delight of the teacher who finds an apt pupil. "Good, good! Now if you believe in the truth of what you say, abandon men with their corrupt customs and their worthless laws. Live in a remote place and follow no law but the law of earth and sky!"

I replied, "Sir, I believe what I say."

He raised his hand and spoke in a voice obdurate and stern, "Belief is one thing, but the deed another. Many are they who speak like the sea, yet their lives are like the swamps. Many are they who raise their heads above the mountain peaks, yet their souls remain slumbering in the darkness of the caves."

While he spoke, I had no chance to interrupt. He rose from his place and laid the thrush upon an old coat near the window. He then took a handful of dry sticks and threw them on the fire, saying, "Take off your shoes and dry your feet. There is nothing so unhealthy to man as damp. Dry your clothes well and do not be bashful."

I went and stood by the fire, steam rising from my sodden clothes, but he stood in the door of the hut, staring at the angry sky.

After a moment, I asked him, "Was it a long time ago that you came to this cell?"

He replied without looking at me, "I came here when the earth was without form, and void; and darkness was upon the face of the deep, and the spirit of God moved upon the face of the waters."

I was silent, but in my heart I thought, "How strange is this man, and how difficult it is to know him as he is. Nonetheless, I must talk with him and learn the mysteries of his spirit. I will wait patiently until he ceases to be disdainful and he becomes softer and gentle."

III

Darkness threw its black cloak upon the valleys, and the rain beat down until I imagined that the Flood had come a second time to destroy life and purify the earth of its filth. The raging storm seemed to produce a peace in Yusof el-Fakhri's soul, for sometimes a cause has a contrary effect. His distaste for me was suddenly transformed into friendship. He rose and lit two candles. He set before me an earthenware jug of wine and a plate of bread, cheese, oil, honey, and dried fruits. He sat down opposite me and said courteously, "This is all the food I have. Please, my brother, share it with me."

We ate our supper in silence, listening to the wail of the wind and the weeping of the rain. I studied his face between bites, searching it for clues hidden in the depths of his soul that might reveal the import of his inclinations and sentiments, the mysteries rooted in his psyche.

After he removed the dinner, he took a copper coffeepot out of the fire, poured pure, fragrant coffee into two cups, and opened a box of cigarettes. Quietly he said, "Please, my brother."

I took a cigarette and picked up the coffee cup. I could scarcely believe what my eyes saw. He was looking at me as though he heard my thoughts, smiling and shaking his head. After I had lit a cigarette and drunk a little coffee, he said, "Naturally, you are surprised to find wine, tobacco, and coffee in this cell, and by the food and bedding. I do not blame you, for you, like many, imagine that isolation from men means isolation from life and from the natural pleasures and simple delights of life."

I replied, "Yes, sir, for we are accustomed to think that one who turns away from the world to worship God leaves behind all the pleasures and delights of the world to live a rude, ascetic, and solitary life, contenting himself with water and herbs."

He said, "I might have worshipped God when I was among people, for worship does not require isolation and solitude. I did not abandon the world to find God, for I had found him in the house of my father and in every other place. I fled from men because my character was not compatible with their characters, my dreams did not agree with their dreams. I abandoned men because I found myself a wheel turning to the right among many wheels turning to the left. I left the city because I found it a diseased tree, ancient and strong, with roots deep in the darkness of the earth and branches rising beyond the clouds, but whose flowers were ambition, evil, and crime, whose fruits were care, affliction, and woe. Some of the righteous sought to graft onto it what would change its nature, but they did not succeed. They died despairing, oppressed, and defeated."

At that, he leaned toward the hearth, seeming to find pleasure in the influence his words had upon me. He raised his voice a little and continued: "No, I do not seek solitude for prayer and asceticism, for prayer is the song of the heart and will reach the ears of God even if it is mixed with the voices of millions. Asceticism? It controls the body and mortifies its desires. This has no place in my religion. God fashioned bodies as temples for spirits. We must protect these temples so that they may remain strong and pure, suitable for divinity to descend into them.

"No, my brother, I do not seek solitude for prayer and asceticism. I sought it as I fled from men, from their laws and teachings and customs and thoughts, from their clamor and cries. I sought solitude so that I would not see the faces of men who sell their souls to buy that which is less than their souls in worth and honor. I sought solitude that I might not meet women who go about with necks outstretched, eyes winking, upon their mouths a thousand smiles, and in the depths of their hearts a single purpose. I sought solitude so that I would not have to sit with those who, having only partial knowledge, see the image of a science in a dream and imagine themselves in wisdom's inner circle. While alert and wakeful, they see one apparition of reality and imagine that they possess its perfect essence. I sought loneliness because I had wearied of the boorish courtesy that imagined refinement to be weakness, forbearance to be cowardice, arrogance to be a kind of glory.

"I sought loneliness because I was weary of the rich, who think that suns and moons and stars rise only from their treasures and set only in their pockets; weary of the statesmen who play games with the hopes of nations and who leave gold dust in their eyes and fill their ears with the echoes of words. I was weary of the priests who exhorted men with counsels that they themselves did not follow, asking of others what they did not expect of themselves. I sought loneliness and solitude because I had received nothing from human hands save that whose price my heart had paid. I sought loneliness and isolation because I loathed that great and awful palace called civilization, that building with its fine architecture standing upon a hill of human skulls.

"I sought solitude because in solitude is a life of spirit and thought, of heart and body. I sought the wilderness because there I found the light of the sun, the scent of flowers, the melodies of brooks. I sought the mountains because there I found the awakening of spring, the desires of summer, the songs of autumn, and the energy of winter. I came to this lonely cell because I wished to know the secrets of the earth and to draw near to the throne of God."

He fell silent, breathing deeply, as though he had thrown a heavy burden off his back. His eyes flashed with a strange and magical light. Pride and willfulness and power shone on his face.

I watched him for a few minutes, pleased at the discovery of that which had been hidden from me. Then I addressed him, "You are correct in all that you say, but, sir, can you not see? You have diagnosed the ills and diseases of society and have demonstrated to me that you are one of its skilled physicians. It is not right for the physician to leave before the patient is cured or dead. The world has a pressing need for men like you. It is unjust for you to separate yourself from the people when you are able to assist them."

He stared at me for a moment, then said in a voice filled with despair and bitterness, "From the beginning the physicians have attempted to save the sick from their sickness. Some have used scalpels, and others drugs and powders. All these physicians have died without hope or expectation. Woe to the patient who, throughout the ages, has had no choice but to confine himself to his filthy bed, befriended only by his unhealing sores! Yet when someone visited him to nurse his wounds, he reached out his hands to strangle him. The truth that enrages me and turns my blood to fire is that this evil patient murders the physician, then closes his eyes and says to himself, 'In truth, he was a great physician . . .' No, my brother, there is no one among men who can help them. However skilled the husbandman may be, he cannot make his field to blossom in the midst of winter."

I answered him thus, "Sir, the winter of the world shall pass, and after it shall come the bright and beautiful spring. The flowers shall bloom in the fields and the brooks sing in the valleys!"

He frowned and sighed, saying in a voice tinged with sadness, "Would that I knew whether God has divided the life of mankind, which is all eternity, into seasons like the seasons of the year, evanescent and following each other in succession. After a million years, will a nation of men appear upon the face of the earth living by the spirit and the truth? Will a time come when man will sit in glory at the right hand of life, delighting in the brilliance of the day and the calm of night? Will what you foresee come to pass? Or will it come to pass only after the earth is sated with the flesh of men, has quenched its thirst with their blood?"

He stood up, raising his right hand as though he were pointing to a world other than this. "Those are implausible dreams, and this cell is not a house of dreams. That which I know with certainty fills every corner and space in it, fills indeed every place in these valleys and these mountains. But what I know with certainty is only this: I am an existent being, and in the depths of my being is hunger and thirst. I know this truth—that I serve the bread and wine of life in vessels that I have made with my own hand. For that reason I left the banquet tables of men and came to this place. Here I shall remain to the end."

He walked back and forth in the room as I reflected on him and pondered his words and what might have caused him to paint a picture of mankind in such crooked lines and dark colors. I interrupted him to ask, "How can I respect your ideas and purposes, sir, or respect your solitude and isolation, when I know—and the knowledge brings sorrow—that by your renunciation and self-exile this wretched nation has lost a gifted man capable of serving and awakening her?"

Shaking his head, he replied, "This nation is no different than all other nations. All men have the same nature. They differ, one from another, only on the surface and in their innumerable exterior appearances. The wretchedness of the Oriental nations is the wretchedness of all the earth. There is nothing in the West that you can consider superior except yet another manifestation of empty delusion. Hypocrisy remains hypocrisy, even when its talons are manicured. Corruption remains corruption, even when its touch is soft. A lie does not become truth by dressing in silk and living in castles. Fraud does not become honesty by riding in trains or ascending to the sky in airships. Greed will not become contentment by surveying or weighing the elements. Crimes will not become virtues by traveling among factories and laboratories.

"Then there is slavery—slavery to life, slavery to teachings and customs and fashions, slavery to the dead. It will remain slavery even if its face is painted and its dress is changed. Slavery will remain slavery even if it calls itself freedom. No, my brother, the Westerner is no higher than the Oriental, nor is the Oriental more debased than the Westerner. They are no more different than the wolf is from the hyena. I have looked for myself and seen that behind the varying manifestations of human society is a single just law distributing misery, blindness, and ignorance equally. It does not distinguish one people from another or treat one group unjustly and not another."

Astonished and baffled, I said, "Then is civilization and all that is in it is vanity?"

In excitement he replied, "Yes, civilization is vanity, and all that is in it is vanity. What are these inventions and discoveries except vices by which the mind distracts itself in moments of boredom and discontent? Shortening distances, leveling mountains, controlling the seas and the air—all are false fruits made of smoke. They will neither please the eye nor nourish the heart nor exalt the soul. As for the riddles and enigmas that they name 'sciences' and 'arts', they are nothing but golden shackles and chains that men drag, delighting in their glitter and the jingling of their links. No, they are cages whose bars and wires man began to forge in ancient times, little knowing that the end of his efforts would be to make himself a captive imprisoned within them.

"Yes, the deeds of man are vanity, and vanity his every goal, desire, wish, purpose, and hope. Everything upon the earth is vanity. Among all the vanities of life there is but one thing fit for the soul, fit to be passionately desired. There is nothing but a single thing."

I said, "What is that, sir?"

He stood silent for a moment, his eyes shut, his face shining and happy. In a sweet and trembling voice he said, "It is wakefulness of the soul. It is wakefulness in the depths of the depths of the soul. It is a thought bringing sudden ecstasy in a heedless moment, clearing one's vision so that one sees life surrounded by songs, encircled by halos, raised up like a tower of light between earth and infinity. It is one of the candles of the innermost essence of existence breaking suddenly into flame within the spirit and burning away the chaff, floating, fluttering in the broad sky. It is an affection descending into an individual's heart: he rises, astonished, and rejects all that is opposed to it, hating all that fails to conform to it, rebelling against those who do not comprehend its mystery. It is the hidden hand that ripped the veil from before my eyes at a moment when I was in the company of family, friends, and fellow-countrymen: I arose bewildered and baffled, saying to myself, 'Whose faces are these, and who are these people staring at me? How do they know me? Where did I meet them? Why am I standing among them? Rather, why am I sitting among them and conversing with them? Am I a stranger among them, or are they strangers in the houses that life built for me and whose keys life entrusted to me?'"

He was suddenly silent, as though recollection were drawing forms and shapes in his memory that he did not wish to reveal. Then he spread his arms and whispered, "This happened to me four years ago. I abandoned the world and came to this empty land to live in wakefulness, to take my pleasures from thought, affection, and silence."

He walked to the door of the cell and looked into the depths of the night, then he shouted as though he were speaking to the storm, "It is a wakefulness in the depths of the soul, and whoever knows it is unable to reveal it with speech. Whoever does not know it, no, he cannot apprehend its mysteries."

IV

A long hour passed in whispered thoughts and shouts at the storm. Yusof el-Fakhri sometimes paced back and forth in the middle of the room and sometimes stood at the door, staring at that grim sky. And I? I remained silent, observing the waves pounding in his spirit, trying to comprehend his words, pondering his life and, beyond his life, the pleasures and hurts of solitude. When the second part of the night reached an end, he came near me and looked into my face for a long time, as though he were trying to preserve in his memory a drawing of the man to whom he had exposed the mystery of his solitude and isolation. Then he slowly said, "Now I am going out to walk in the storm. It is a habit that gives me pleasure in the autumn and winter. . . Here are the coffeepot and the cigarettes. If you should want wine, you will find it in the jar. If you want to sleep, you will find blankets and pillows in the corner."

As he said this, he put on a rough black coat and smiled, "I hope that you will shut the door of the cell when you go in the morning. I plan to spend all day tomorrow in the Cedars."

He went to the door and picked up a long staff that leaned next to it. He said, "Should a storm surprise you a second time when you are in this neighborhood, do not hesitate to seek refuge in this cell. But I hope that your soul will love the storms, not fear them . . . Good evening, my brother."

He went quickly out into the night. When I stepped to the door of the cell to see which direction he had gone, the darkness had swallowed him. I remained a few minutes listening to his footsteps in the gravel of the valley.

Morning came and the storm had passed. The clouds dispersed and the rocks and forests appeared, clothed in the light of the sun. I left the cell, closing the door after me. In my soul I felt something of that spiritual wakefulness of which Yusof el-Fakhri had spoken.

Before I returned to the abodes of men, before I saw their movements and heard their voices, I stopped and said in my heart, "Yes, spiritual wakefulness is befitting to man—rather, it is the goal of being—but is not civilization, with its obscurities and ambiguities, one of the causes of spiritual awakening? I wonder how we are able to deny an existent thing when its very existence is evidence for the truth of its right? Perhaps modern civilization is a passing accident, but the eternal law may make accidents a stairway whose steps reach to the absolute substance."

I never again talked to Yusof el-Fakhri, for at the end of that autumn life took me away from the north of Lebanon. I went as an exile to distant lands, where storms were dark. But in those countries asceticism is a kind of madness.

The Poet

I am a stranger in this world.

I am a stranger.
In my exile there is a grim isolation and a painful loneliness.

Yet it makes me ever think of a magical homeland that I do not know.

Exile peoples my dreams with phantoms of a distant land that my eyes have not seen.

I am a stranger to my family and to my friends.
Should I meet one of them, I say in my soul, "Who is that? How do I know him? What law is it that links me with him? How am I related to him, and why do I associate with him?"

I am a stranger to my soul.

When I hear my tongue speak, my ear is startled by my voice, and I see my hidden essence laughing and crying, fearless and terrified.

My being is astonished at my being, and my spirit seeks the meaning of my spirit.

But I, I remain hidden, concealed, hedged about with mists, cloaked in silence.

I am a stranger to my body.

When I stop before a mirror, I see features that I do not know, I see in my eyes what is hidden nowhere in my depths.

I walk the streets of the city, and the boys follow me jeering, "He is blind! Let us give him a cane to lean upon."

In haste I flee from them, only to meet a swarm of girls clinging to my clothes and shouting,

"He is as deaf as the stones. Let us fill his ears with songs of flirtation and love."

I run to escape them and meet a group of young men. They stand around me and say, "He is mute like the tomb. Let us untangle his knotted tongue!"

So in fear I leave them and encounter a party of old men, pointing at me with trembling fingers.

"He is mad. His reason was destroyed
in the land of genies and ghouls.

∽

I am a stranger in this world.

I am a stranger wandering the east of the world
and the west.

I have found nowhere to lay my head, nor have I
met one who recognizes me or would listen to me.

When I wake in the morning, I find myself a
prisoner in a dark cave, vipers hanging from its roof
and vermin scuttling in its corners.

When I go out to the light, the image of my body
follows me and the imaginings of my soul go before
me, leading me I know not where, calling me to that
which I comprehend not, clinging to things of which
I have no need.

When evening comes, I lie down upon my mat
of ostrich feathers and thorns.

Strange thoughts obsess me and desires, disquieting then delightful, painful then pleasant.

At midnight phantoms of ages past, spirits of
forgotten nations, come to me from the crevasses of
the cave.

I stare at them, and they stare at me.

I speak to them, seeking to understand, and they answer, smiling.

I try to seize them but they vanish like smoke in the wind.

∾

I am a stranger in this world.

I am a stranger, and no one in the world of being knows a single word of the language of my soul.

I wander in the empty wilderness and see the brooks bubbling up and leaping from the depths of the valley to the mountain peak.

I see the bare trees burst into leaf, flower, bear fruit, and shed their leaves, all in a single moment.

Then their branches fall down in decay to become like wiggling speckled snakes.

I see the birds soaring upwards and descending, trilling and shrieking.

They land and open their wings, metamorphosed into naked women, their hair unbound, their heads held high, looking at me with love from behind eyelids painted with kohl, smiling at me with lips like honeyed roses, reaching to me with soft fair hands scented with myrrh and frankincense.

Then they shudder and hide themselves from my gaze, disappearing like mist, leaving their laughter echoing in the air to mock and scorn me.

∾

I am a stranger in this world.

I am a poet.

I write in verse life's prose, and in prose life's verse.

Thus I am a stranger, and will remain a stranger until death snatches me away and carries me to my homeland.

A Vision

There in the midst of a field at the edge of a crystal brook I saw a cage, its bars fashioned by a skilled hand. In a corner of the cage was a dead sparrow, in another a dry water-dish and a cup empty of seed.

I stopped, seized by silence, and shrank back to listen, as though the dead bird and the sound of the stream contained a warning addressed to the conscience, conveying meaning to the heart. Pondering, I realized that the unhappy sparrow had met death by thirst, though he was beside running waters. Hunger had destroyed him, though he was in the midst of the fields that are the cradle of life. He was like a rich man, locked in his treasuries, dying of hunger, surrounded by gold.

After a moment the cage was suddenly transformed into the diaphanous skeleton of a man. The dead bird had become a human heart. Scarlet blood dripped from a deep wound. The edges of the wound were shaped like the lips of a grieving woman.

Then I heard a voice emerging from the wound with the drops of blood, "I am the human heart, a prisoner of matter and murdered by the laws of man, who is made of clay. In the midst of a beautiful field, at the edge of the springs of life, I am imprisoned in a cage of laws made by man to bind the emotions. In a cradle of the good things of creation, placed in front of love, I died neglected, for the fruits of those good things, the results of that love, were forbidden to me. All that would give me joy was declared shameful, and all that I would desire they decreed humiliation.

"I am the human heart. I was imprisoned in the darkness of the laws of society, and I became weak. I was bound with chains of delusion, and I died. I was neglected in the corners of the city's sin, and I perished. The tongue of humanity was still and its eyes were dry, and it was smiling."

I heard these words and saw them coming from that wounded heart with the drops of blood. After that I saw nothing more and heard no voice, but returned to my own reality.

Slavery

Men are but slaves of life. This slavery hedges in their days with misery and debasement and floods their nights with tears and blood.

Seven thousand years have passed since I first was born, yet I have seen only submissive slaves and shackled prisoners.

I have traveled the East and the West of the world and wandered in the shadows of life and in its bright days. I have beheld the caravans of nations and peoples journeying from its caves to its castles, but until now I have seen only serfs bowed beneath their burdens, arms bound by chains, knees bent before idols.

I have followed man's path from Babylon to Paris, from Nineveh to New York. Everywhere beside his footprints in the sand I saw the marks of his dragging chains. Everywhere the valleys and hills echoed to the grief of generations and centuries.

I entered the palaces, the squares, the temples. I stood before thrones, altars, and pulpits. I saw the laborer a slave to the merchant, the merchant a slave to the soldier, the soldier a slave to the general, the general a slave to the king, the king a slave to the priest, the priest a slave to the idol, the idol shaped from dust by devils and raised above a hill of dead men's skulls.

I entered the houses of the rich and mighty and the huts of the poor and weak. I stood in halls inlaid with ivory and glowing with gold leaf. I crouched in tenements crowded with the ghosts of despair and the gasps of the dying. I saw babes sucking slavery with their milk, boys learning servility with their letters, girls donning clothing woven of bondage and submissiveness, women sleeping on beds of obedience and compliance.

I followed the generations from the banks of the Congo to the shores of the Euphrates, from the mouth of the Nile to Mount Sinai, from the squares of Athens to the churches of Rome, from the alleys of Constantinople to the great buildings of London. Everywhere I saw slavery being carried in processions toward the altars and being called 'god.' They poured libations of wine and perfume at its feet and called it 'angel.' They burned incense before its images and called it 'prophet.' They

fell down prostrate before it and called it 'the holy law.'
They fought and killed for it and called it 'patriotism.'
They submitted to its will and called it the 'shadow of
God on earth.' Then they burned their houses and razed
their buildings at its will and called it 'fraternity' and
'equality.' They strove then and made every effort for it,
calling it 'wealth' and 'trade.' Indeed, it has many names
and but one reality, many manifestations of a single sub-
stance. It is a single disease, eternal without beginning,
without end, appearing with many contradictory symp-
toms and differing sores, inherited from the fathers by
the sons as they inherit the breath of life. The ages receive
its seeds in the soil of the ages, just as the seasons reap
what the seasons have sown.

∾

How strange are the species and varieties of sla-
very that I have encountered:

Blind slavery, the slavery of men of the present
trusting in the past of their fathers, kneeling in blind
imitation of the customs of their grandfathers, mak-
ing themselves new bodies for old spirits, whitewashed
tombs for bleached bones.

Dumb slavery, the slavery in which the days of a
man are bound to the skirts of a woman he despises,
in which the body of a woman is tied to the bed of a

husband who loathes her. Their life is to be strapped onto the two feet of slavery like sandals.

Deaf slavery, the slavery of those individuals compelled to follow the tastes of their environment, to adopt its colors, to dress according to its styles, until their voices become like echoes and their bodies like passing illusions.

Lame slavery, the slavery of the vigorous, their necks bent beneath the yokes of the devious, the ardor of the strong bent to the whims of those greedy for glory and fame, used like tools in their hands until they are dropped and broken.

Hoary slavery, the slavery that descends with the spirits of infants from the broad sky to the abodes of misery where need dwells beside ignorance and misery lives near to despair. They are children in wretchedness. They live their lives in crime, and die in depravity.

Spotted slavery, slavery that buys at unfair prices, that calls things by false names, that calls shrewdness 'intelligence', gossip 'knowledge', weakness 'forbearance', and cowardice 'pride.'

Twisted slavery, slavery that makes the tongues of the weak to prattle in fear, speaking of what they know not, pretending to that which is not in their hearts, becoming like a coat which the hands of poverty roll and unroll.

Hunchbacked slavery, slavery that makes a people subject to the laws of other peoples.

Mangy slavery, slavery by which the sons of kings are crowned kings.

Dark slavery, slavery by which the innocent children of criminals are branded with shame.

Slavery to slavery itself, the power by which it continues.

ॐ

When I tired of following the generations and wearied of watching the processions of peoples and nations, I sat alone in the valley of ghosts, where the memories of past generations were concealed and the spirits of future ages laid in wait. There I saw an emaciated specter walking alone, staring at the face of the Sun. I asked it, "Who are you? What is your name?"

It replied, "My name is Liberty."

I said, "Where are your children?"

It said, "One died crucified, one died mad, and none other was born."

Then it disappeared before my eyes behind the mists.

In the City of the Dead

Yesterday I escaped the tumult of the city and went walking through the quiet fields. I came to a steep hill that nature had dressed in its loveliest finery. I stopped; spread out before me was the city, its lofty buildings and stately palaces shrouded in a thick cloud of factory smoke.

I sat to ponder from a distance the deeds of men. Most acts, I thought, were hardship. I tried not to think in my heart of what the sons of Adam had wrought. I turned my eyes toward the fields, the seat of God's glory. In their midst I saw a cemetery, its marble tombs surrounded by cypress trees.

There, between the city of the living and the city of the dead, I sat in thought. I thought of the constant strife and perpetual motion of the one and of the prevailing calm and enduring rest of the other. In one direction hope and despair, love and hatred, wealth and poverty, faith and denial; in the other dust being transformed within the dust until it is manifested as plant and animal, completed in the silence of the night.

While I was lost in these meditations, my gaze was drawn to a large group of people walking slowly, their music preceding them as they filled the air with sad songs. It was a procession combining stateliness and grandeur, mingling the classes of men, the bier of a rich and powerful man, the mortal remains of the dead followed by the living, cries and wailing, weeping and laments scattering through the air.

They reached the cemetery, and the priests gathered to pray and burn incense. The musicians blew their trumpets. After a while, the eulogists began to speak, praising the departed in the choicest language. Then the poets recited their eloquent elegies, all at wearisome length. Finally the crowd straggled away, leaving behind a tomb for which the masons and the builders had striven to outdo each other, a tomb surrounded by wreaths of flowers arranged by the hands of artists.

The procession turned back toward the city as I watched from a distance in thought.

At that moment I saw two men lifting a wooden coffin. Behind them was a woman dressed in rags, carrying on her hip a suckling child, by her side a dog. Sometimes it looked at her, sometimes at the coffin. It was the bier of a poor and humble man. Behind it followed a wife weeping in grief, a babe crying for the tears of his mother, a faithful dog. Its path was sadness and agony.

When they reached the cemetery, they laid the coffin in a grave far from the marble tombs. Then they went away in pathetic silence. Until they disappeared from my sight behind the trees, the dog kept looking back towards the place where lay his friend.

Then I looked toward the city of the living and said in my soul, "That is for the rich and the powerful." Then I looked toward the city of the dead and said, "This, too, is for the rich and powerful. O Lord, where is the homeland of the poor and the weak?"

As I said this, I looked toward the thick clouds, tinged with gold at the edges from the rays of the beautiful sun, and I heard a voice within me say, "There!"

To My
Oppressed Friend

O you who were born on the bed of misery, nourished at the breast of debasement, who played as a child in the houses of tyranny, you who eat your stale bread with sighs and drink your muddy water mixed with bitter tears.

O soldier ordered by the unjust laws of men to leave his wife, his small children, his friends, and enter the arena of death for the sake of ambition, which they call 'necessity.'

O poet who lives as a stranger in his homeland, unknown among those who know him, who desires only to live on crumbs and of the vanities of the world asks only ink and paper.

O prisoner thrown into darkness because of a small offense made a great crime by those who requite evil with evil, banished by the wise who would establish the right by means of the wrong.

And you, O unfortunate woman, to whom God has given beauty. A faithless youth saw it and followed you, beguiled you, overcame your poverty with gold. When you submitted to him, he abandoned you. You are like prey trembling in the talons of debasement and wretchedness.

And you, my humble friends, martyrs to the laws of man. You are wretched, and your wretchedness is the result of the outrages of the mighty, of the injustice of the judge, of the tyranny of the rich, and of the selfishness of the slave to his desires.

Do not despair, for beyond the injustices of this world, beyond matter, beyond the clouds, beyond the æther, beyond all things is a power which is all justice, all kindness, all tenderness, all love.

You are like flowers that grow in the shadow. Soon gentle breezes will blow and carry your seeds into the light of the Sun where they will live a life of beauty.

You are like the naked trees weighed down with the snows of winter. Soon the spring shall come to clothe you with green and succulent leaves.

Truth shall rend the veil of tears concealing your smiles.

Brethren, I welcome you and I despise your oppressors.

The Cry
of the Graves

The Emir mounted the throne of judgment. The wise men of his city sat to his right and left, their creased faces the reflection of their books and treatises. The soldiers were arrayed around him, their swords drawn and their spears raised. The people stood before him, some drawn by curiosity to watch, others awaiting the judgment of a relative's crime, but all had bowed their heads and averted their gaze. They held their breaths as though the eyes of the Emir had the power to strike terror into their souls and hearts. Finally, the audience was over and the hour of judgment came. The Emir raised his hand and called out, "Bring the criminals before me, one by one, and tell me of their misdeeds and offences."

The gate of the prison was opened, revealing the gloomy walls within. It was like looking down the throat of a ravenous beast. From inside came the rattling of fetters and chains and the despairing cries of the prisoners. The onlookers turned to look and stretched as though they were about to see death's prey emerging from the depths of that tomb.

After a moment two soldiers emerged from the prison leading a youth, his arms in manacles. His unhappy face and agonized features told of a high spirit and brave heart. They placed him in the center of the court and stepped back a little toward the crowd. The Emir stared at him for a minute, then asked, "What is the crime of this man who stands before us with his head held high, as though he were in a place of honor, and not in the dock of justice?"

One of his servants answered him, "He is an evil murderer. Yesterday he resisted an officer traveling to the villages on the Emir's business. He struck the officer to the ground and overpowered him. The sword dripping with the blood of the murdered man was still in his hand."

The Emir rose from his throne in wrath. His eyes flashed with anger. He shouted in his loudest voice, "Return him to the darkness and weigh down his body with fetters. When dawn comes tomorrow, strike off his head with a sword. Dump his body outside the city to be eaten by vultures and wild animals. Let the wind carry his stench to his family and all who might love him."

The youth was led back to the prison, and the people watched him with pity and deep sighs, for he was a young man in the spring of life, handsome and strongly built.

The two soldiers led out another prisoner, this time a lovely and fragile girl. A pall of profound despair had marred the fair features of her face. Her eyes were red with weeping. Grief and remorse weighed upon her neck.

The Emir looked at her and said, "What has this emaciated woman done? She stands before me scarcely more than the shadow beside her."

One of the soldiers replied, "She is an adulteress. Her husband came to her suddenly by night and found her in the arms of her lover. He turned her over to the police, but her companion escaped."

The Emir stared at her. Her head was bowed in shame. It was with force and severity that he spoke: "Stretch her on a carpet of thorns, that she might remember the bed that she disgraced with her offence. Give her vinegar to drink mixed with bitter herbs, to remind her of the taste of forbidden lips. When dawn comes, lead her naked from the city and stone her. Leave her body there, that her flesh might give pleasure to wolves and her bones be gnawed by maggots and flies."

The girl vanished back into the darkness of the prison. The onlookers stared at her, marveling at the justice of the Emir and pitying the beauty of her sorrow-stricken face and her unhappy eyes.

The two soldiers appeared a third time dragging an older man. His shaking legs trailed behind him along the ground like two strips torn from the hem of his shirt. He glanced apprehensively in all directions, his eyes ghosts of suffering, poverty, and wretchedness.

The Emir looked at him, and said in a voice of disgust, "What is the crime of this filth standing like a dead man among the living?"

One of the soldiers answered, "He is no more than a thief. He broke into the church at night, but the pious monks seized him. In his shirt they found chalices from their holy altars."

The Emir stared at him like a hungry hawk at a broken-winged sparrow. He shouted, "Take him down into the depths of darkness and shackle him with steel. When dawn comes, drag him to a tall tree and hang him with linen rope. Leave his body to hang between earth and sky. The elements shall scatter his larcenous fingers and the winds shall break his members into fragments."

They took the thief back to prison, and the people whispered into each other's ears, "How could this weak sinner dare to steal chalices from the holy monastery?"

The Emir descended from the throne of judgment, followed by the wise men and the lawyers. The soldiers marched before and after him. The crowd of spectators dispersed. The square emptied of all but the shrieks of the prisoners, and the moans of the despairing flickered like shadows upon the walls.

I stood watching like a mirror placed before moving shapes, reflecting on the laws with which man has burdened man, pondering that which men reckon to be just, delving into the mysteries of life, investigating the meaning of being. In the end my thoughts blurred like the sun sinking into the mists, so I left that place, saying to myself, "The grasses suck in the elements of the soil, and the sheep devour the grass. The wolves prey on the sheep, and the rhinoceros slays the wolf. The lion hunts the rhinoceros, and death destroys the lion. Is there any power that can defeat death and convert this chain of iniquities into eternal justice? Is there any power that can transmute these loathsome causes into comely effects? Is there any power that can grasp all the elements of life and unite them with itself in joy, as the sea unites all the streams in song in its depths? Is there any power that can bring the murderer and his victim, the adulteress and her lover, the thief and his booty before a court more splendid and lofty than the judgment of the Emir?"

II

The next day I left the city and went walking in the fields, a place where the breath of silence rejoices the soul, where the purity of the air kills the germs of despair and the hopelessness bred by narrow streets and dark houses. When I reached the edge of the valley, I saw flocks of carrion birds rising and falling, filling the air with their screeching and screams and the rustling of their wings. I went toward them to investigate. I saw a man's corpse hanging from a tall tree, the corpse of a naked woman fallen on the ground, stoned to death, and the corpse of a youth, his blood mixed with the dust, his severed head lying apart.

I stood there, the horror of the scene blinding me with a dark and opaque veil. Nothing could I see but the image of horrible death standing among corpses splattered with blood. I could hear nothing save the mourning cries of nothingness mixed with the screeches of the carrion birds hovering over the prey given them by the laws of men.

Three children of Adam, who yesterday were hugged to the breast of life today were in the grip of death.

Three who, according to the customs of men, had offended justice, so blind Law had stretched forth its hand to crush them without pity.

Three whom ignorance had made criminals because they were weak, so the Law killed them because it was strong.

A man slays another man, so men say, "This is a wicked murderer." When the Emir slays him, men say, "This is a just Emir."

A man tries to steal from the monastery, and men say, "He is an evil thief." The Emir steals his life, and they say, "This is a virtuous Emir."

A woman betrays her husband, and men say, "She is an adulterous whore." But when the Emir strips her naked and stones her to death before witnesses, they say, "He is a high-minded Emir."

To shed blood is forbidden, but who made it licit for the Emir?

To steal property is a crime, but who made it a virtue to rob people of their spirits?

To betray a husband is despicable, but who made stoning bodies praiseworthy?

Do we requite a sin with a greater sin and say, "This is the Holy Law"? Do we fight corruption with wider corruption and call out, "This is the statute"?

Do we oppose crime with more serious crime and cry, "This is Justice"?

Has not the Emir destroyed an enemy in his life? Has he not stolen money or land from some one of his helpless subjects? Has he not seduced a beautiful woman? Is he so free from these sins that he can execute the murderer, hang the thief, and stone the adulteress?

Who are they who hanged this thief on this tree? Are they angels come down from heaven, or are they only men who embezzle and steal whatever their hands can seize?

And who cut off the head of this murderer? Are they Prophets come down from on high, or are they only soldiers who murder and shed blood wherever they may?

And who stoned this adulteress? Are they pure ascetics come from their cells, or are they only men of the flesh who commit sins and practice vileness under the concealing curtain of night?

The Holy Law—what is this Holy Law? Who saw it coming down with the light of the Sun from the farthest reaches of the sky? Which creature of the flesh sees into the heart of God and learns His will for man? In what age did angels walk among men to say, "Forbid the weak from the light of life, and slay those who fall short with edge of the sword, and trample the sinners yet again"?

Such thoughts continued to jostle in my mind and to vie for my sympathies. Then I heard the sound of footsteps nearby. I saw a girl appear from among the trees and cautiously approach the three corpses, glancing in fear in all directions. When she saw the severed head of the youth, she screamed in horror. She knelt down beside it and took it in her trembling arms. Tears poured from her eyes. She stroked the curls of his hair with her fingertips and sobbed in a deep, tormented voice that rose from the depths of her heart. When she was worn out from weeping and grief, she began hastily to dig in the earth with her hands. When she had dug a deep enough grave, she dragged the dead youth to it and slowly laid him there, placing his bloodstained head between his hands. After she had covered him with earth, she planted at the head of his grave the blade of the sword that had cut off his head.

When she turned to leave, I approached her. She started, trembling in fear, then stood with her head bowed, hot tears raining from her eyes. In a whisper she said, "Denounce me to the Emir if you wish. It would be better for me to die and be rejoined to one who freed me from the hand of shame than to have left his body as food for the carrion birds and the wild beasts."

I replied, "You need not fear me, unfortunate woman, for I lamented the fate of your youth before you. Rather, tell me how he rescued you from the hand of shame."

She said, choking on her words, "The Emir's officer came to our fields to collect the crop and poll taxes. When he saw me, he looked at me with hidden satisfaction and levied a tax on my father's field so heavy that a rich man would have been unable to pay it. He seized me to take me to the palace of the Emir in place of the gold. In tears I begged for mercy but he paid me no mind. I pleaded that my father was an old man, but he had no mercy. At last I screamed for help to the men of the village. This youth, my betrothed, came and rescued me from those brutal hands. The officer burned with rage and attacked him. The youth outran him and snatched an old sword that was hanging on the wall. He struck at the officer, defending his own life and my honor. Being an upright man, he did not flee like a murderer but waited, standing near the body of the officer until the soldiers came and led him to the jail in irons."

As she said this, she looked at me with an expression that would melt the heart, then turned hastily away, the echoes of her agonized cries setting the æther to tremble and shake.

A moment later I saw a youth in the spring of life approaching, his face concealed by his cloak. When he reached the body of the adulterous woman, he stopped, took off his cloak, and covered her naked limbs with it. He began digging in the dirt with a knife he had brought. Then he quietly placed her in the hole, pouring dust over her to hide her, each handful mixed with a tear dropped from his eyelashes. When he had finished his task, he picked some of the flowers that were growing there and arranged them carefully over the grave. As he started to leave, I stopped him and said, "What connection has this fallen woman with you that you would dare to defy the will of the Emir and endanger your own life to protect her broken body from the circling carrion birds?"

He looked at me, his eyelids, swollen from weeping and lack of sleep, telling of the intensity of his grief and tortured love. In a strangled voice accompanied by pained sighs, he said, "I am that wretched man for whose sake she was stoned. I loved her and she loved me since we were small children playing among the houses. As we grew up, love grew between us until it became an absolute master whom we served with the affections of our two hearts. Love drew us to him and we venerated him in our innermost spirits, and he embraced us.

"One day when I was gone from the city, her father forced her to marry a man she hated. When I returned and heard this news, my days were turned to long and pitch-dark nights. My life became a bitter and continuous struggle. I continued to wrestle with my affections and oppose my own inclinations, but at last they ruled me as the sighted man rules the blind. I went secretly to my beloved, my hope being no more than to see the light of her eyes and hear the music of her voice. I found her alone, lamenting her fate and mourning her days. I sat with her. Silence was our conversation and chastity our third. An hour had not passed when her husband came back unexpectedly. When he saw me, he was filled with impure ideas. He seized her smooth neck in his rough hands and cried in his loudest voice, 'Come see the adulteress and her lover!'

The neighbors came rushing in. The soldiers came to see what had happened, and he gave her into their harsh hands. They led her away, her hair unbound, her clothing torn. But as for me, no one touched me to do me any harm, for blind law and unjust customs punish the woman whenever she falls but are indulgent to the man."

The youth went back toward the city, concealing his face in his clothing. I remained behind, staring thoughtfully and sadly at the hanging corpse of the thief. It swayed a little as the wind disturbed the branches of the tree, its motion a plea to the spirits of the sky that it be cut down and laid upon the breast of the earth next to the one slain for chivalry and the martyr of love.

After an hour a woman appeared, weak in body and dressed in rags. She stood near the hanged man, beating her breast and weeping. Then she climbed the tree and cut the rope with her teeth. The dead man fell to the earth like a wet cloth. The woman climbed down, dug a grave near the other two, and placed him in it. After she had covered him with dirt, she took two pieces of wood, made a cross of them, and planted them at his head. When she turned to go back in the direction she had come from, I stopped her and said, "Woman, what would bequile you into coming to bury a thief and a burglar?"

She stared at me with eyes shadowed by agony and torment. "He was my good husband, my loving companion, and the father of my children—five children, writhing with hunger, the eldest of them eight and the youngest nursing and not yet weaned. My husband was not a thief. He was a farmer tilling the land of the monastery, but he had no profit from it, for the monks gave him only a loaf, which we divided in the evening, and no morsel of it remained in the morning.

"From the time he was a boy, he watered the fields of the monastery with the sweat of his brow and cultivated the strength of his arms in their orchards. When he weakened and the years of toil had stolen his powers and diseases fought for his body, they expelled him, saying, 'The monastery has no more need of you. Now go, and when your sons are grown, send them to us to fill your place in the field.' He wept and made me to weep. He pleaded in the name of Jesus. He entreated them by the angels and the saints, but they had no mercy on him and showed no pity on him or on me or on our naked and hungry children. So he went away and sought work in the city. He came back rejected, for the dwellers in those palaces would only employ strong youths. Then he sat in the middle of the road begging, but the people did not think well of him, but only passed by and said, 'Alms ought not to be given to the apathetic and lazy.'

"One night when we had become so destitute that our children lay too weak from hunger to move and the infant sucked at my breast but found no milk, my husband's features changed. He crept out of the house in the dark and entered one of the monastery's vaults where the monks store the grain from the fields and the wine from the vineyard. He placed a basket of flour on his back and started back to us. He had gone only a few steps when the priests awoke from their sleep and seized him, pouring abuse upon him, both words and blows. When morning came, they handed him over to the soldiers, saying, 'He is a wicked thief who came to steal the golden vessels of the monastery.' The soldiers led him away to the jail and then to the gallows for the carrion birds to fill their bellies with his flesh—only because he sought to fill the bellies of his hungry children from the abundance of grain, that he had harvested with his toil when he was a servant of the monastery."

The poor woman left. From her desperate words unhappy ghosts arose and were carried quickly in all directions, like columns of smoke blown by the wind.

∾

I stood by those three graves like a speechless eulogist, struck dumb by grief, flowing tears giving voice to emotions. I tried to think and reflect, but my soul disobeyed me, for the soul is like a flower that gathers its petals to itself when darkness comes, not giving its breaths to the phantoms of the night.

As I stood there, a cry of oppression poured forth from the grains of earth of those graves like fog pouring from the mouths of valleys. It vibrated in my ears and inspired my words.

I stood silent. If men could understand what the silence says, they would be nearer to the gods and farther from the rapacious beasts of the forest.

I stood sighing. Had the flames of my sighs touched them, the trees of that field would have lurched, left their places, and marched in battalions to fight with their branches against the Emir and his armies, their trunks toppling the walls of the monastery upon the heads of the monks.

I stood staring, stares in which the sweetness of pity and the bitterness of grief poured out over those new graves. The grave of a youth who paid with his life defending the honor of a weak and chaste girl and who rescued her from the claws of a ravening wolf. They cut off his head to repay him for his courage. The girl had sheathed his sword in the dust of his grave that it might remain as a sign speaking plainly beneath the Sun of the fate of manliness in a land where injustice and ignorance rule.

The grave of a girl. Love touched her soul, but her body was subject to the desires of others. She was stoned because her heart insisted on being faithful until death. Her beloved fashioned a bouquet of wild-flowers to lay above her lifeless body. As they wilt and fade, they will tell of souls purified by love and their fate at the hands of a people ruled by matter and struck dumb by ignorance.

The grave of a poor and unfortunate man, his arms made weak by toil in the monastery fields. The monks expelled him, that his arms might be replaced by others. He sought to work for his children's bread but found no work. Then he begged for it but was given nothing. When despair drove him to take back a little of the harvest gathered by his toil and the sweat of his brow, they seized and attacked him. His wife raised a cross over his grave. It will bear witness in the silence of the night beneath the stars to the tyranny of the monks. They have changed the teachings of the Nazarene into swords slashing at necks, the sharp edges cutting the bodies of the poor and weak.

After that the sun disappeared in twilight, as though it were weary of the cares of men and loathed their oppression. The evening began to weave a delicate veil from threads of dark and stillness and spread it over the body of nature. I raised my eyes to the zenith of heaven and spread my arms toward the graves and the symbols upon them. In my loudest voice I cried, "This is your sword, O courage. It is sheathed in the dust. These are your flowers, O love.

Fires have seared them. This is your cross, O Jesus of Nazareth. The darkness of night has covered it."

Between
Night and Morn

Silence, my heart, for the sky does not hear.

Silence, for the æther is burdened with cries of grief. It will not bear your melodies and songs.

Silence, for the ghosts of night do not heed your whispered secrets, and the shadowy processions do not stop before your dreams.

Silence, my heart. Be silent until morn, for he who watches for the morn in patience will meet the morn in strength. He who loves the light is beloved of the light.

Silence, my heart, and hear me speak.

∾

In a dream I saw a thrush singing as it flew over the mouth of a raging volcano.

I saw a lily raise its head above the snows.

I saw a naked houri dancing among the tombs.

I saw a laughing child playing with skulls.

I saw all these forms in a dream. When I awoke and looked about me, I saw the volcano blazing, but I did not hear the thrush singing, nor did I see its flight.

I saw the sky scattering snow upon the fields and valleys, shrouding in white the corpses of the frozen lilies.

I saw the tombs, row upon row, raised before the silence of the ages. But none did I see there swaying in dance nor any bowed in prayer.

I saw a hill of skulls, but none laughed there save the wind.

Awakened, I saw sadness and grief; where had gone the dream's delights and joys?

Why has the splendor of the dream disappeared, and how have its visions vanished? How shall the soul endure until sleep brings back the phantoms of its desires and hopes?

❧

Hearken, my heart, and hear me speak.

Yesterday my soul was a strong and ancient tree, spreading its roots to the depths of the earth and raising its branches toward infinity.

My soul blossomed in spring, bore fruit in summer. In autumn I gathered its fruits in silver bowls and laid them in the midst of the road. Passersby took and ate from them, and went upon their way.

❧

When autumn ended and its hymns of praise turned to dirges and laments, I found that people had left me but a single fruit in the silver bowls.

I took it and ate, and found it bitter like colocynth, sour like unripe grapes.

I said to my soul, "Woe to me, for I have placed a curse in the mouths of men, and in their bellies enmity.

"What have you done, my soul, with the sweetness that your roots have sucked from the bowels of the earth, with the fragrance that your leaves have drunk from the light of the sun?"

Then I uprooted the strong and ancient tree of my soul.

I tore its roots from the clay in which it had sprouted and flourished. I tore its roots from its past, cutting off the memory of a thousand springs and a thousand autumns.

And I planted the tree of my soul once again in another place.

I planted it in a field far distant from the paths of time. I watched by night beside it, saying, "To watch by night brings us near to the stars."

I watered it with my blood and my tears, saying, "There is a fragrance in blood, and in tears a sweetness."

When spring came, my soul blossomed once again.

∾

In summer my soul bore fruit. When autumn came, I gathered its ripened fruits in golden bowls and laid them in the midst of the road. People passed, one by one or in groups, but no one reached out his hand to partake of the offerings.

Then I took a fruit and ate it, found it sweet like the finest honey, succulent like the springs of heaven, delightful as the wine of Babylon, fragrant as the scent of jasmine.

I shouted, "People do not want a blessing in their mouths or truth in their bellies, because a blessing is the daughter of tears and truth the son of blood!"

Then I turned and sat in the shade of the lonely tree of my soul in a field distant from the paths of time.

∾

Silence, my heart, until morn.

Silence, for the sky is revolted by the stench of the dead and cannot drink in your breaths.

Hearken, my heart, and hear me speak.

Yesterday my thought was a ship tossed by the waves of the sea and driven by the winds from shore to shore.

The ship of my thought was empty save for seven cups overflowing with colors, brilliant as the rainbow's hues.

A time came when I wearied of journeying upon the face of the seas and said, "I shall return in the empty ship of my thoughts to the harbor of the city where I was born."

∽

I began to paint the sides of my ship with colors—the yellow of the setting sun, the green of the new spring, the blue of heaven's dome, the red of the dwindling twilight. On its sails and rudder I drew wondrous figures, charming the eye and delighting the sight.

When my work was ended, the ship of my thought was like a prophet's vision, circling in the infinity of sea and sky. I entered the harbor of my city, and the people came out to meet me with thanksgiving and praise. They carried me into the city, beating drums and blowing horns.

This they did because the outside of my ship was decorated brightly, but not a one entered within the ship of my thought.

No one asked what it was that I had carried from beyond the seas.

None knew why I had returned in my empty ship to the harbor.

Then to myself I said, "I have misled the people, and with seven cups of color I have deceived their eyes."

∾

After a year I boarded the ship of my thought and set to sea a second time.

I sailed to the isles of the east, and loaded my ship with myrrh and frankincense, aloes and sandalwood.

I sailed to the isles of the west, and brought back gold dust and ivory, rubies and emeralds, and every precious stone.

From the isles of the north I returned with silk and embroidered and purple cloth.

From the isles of the south I returned with chain mail and sharp swords, tall spears, and weapons of every kind.

I filled the ship of my thought with the treasures and curiosities of the earth and returned to the harbor of my city, saying, "My people shall praise me, but rightly. They will bear me into the city singing and blowing trumpets, but deservedly."

But when I reached the harbor, none came out to meet me. When I entered the streets of the city, none paid me any heed.

I stood in its squares cursing a people to whom I had brought the fruits and treasures of the earth. They stared at me, their mouths full of laughter, mockery on their faces. Then they turned away from me.

∾

I returned to the harbor, dejected and bewildered. No sooner had I seen my ship than I beheld what the struggles and hopes of my journeys had kept from my notice. I cried out.

The waves of the sea had washed the paint from the sides of my ship, leaving naught but bleached bones.

The winds and the gales and the heat of the sun had erased the figures from the sails, leaving them like worn and ash-colored clothes.

I had gathered the curiosities and treasures of the earth into an ark floating upon the face of the waters. I had returned to my people, but they spurned me because their eyes beheld only the external.

In that hour I abandoned the ship of my thought and went to the city of the dead. I sat among the white-washed tombs, thinking of their secrets.

∾

Silence, my heart, until morn.

Silence, for the raging storm scoffs at the whispers of your depths, and the caves of the valley will not echo to the sounds of your voice.

Silence, my heart, until morn. For he who watches patient till the morn, morning will embrace him with ardor.

∾

There! The dawn has broken, my heart. Speak, if you are able to speak!

It is the procession of the morn, my heart! Shall the silence of the night stifle within the depths of your heart songs to greet the morn?

Behold the flocks of dove and thrush scattering through the valley. Shall the horror of the night hinder you from taking wing with them?

The shepherds lead their flocks from corrals and pens.

Shall the ghosts of the night hinder you from following them to the verdant meadows?

The boys and girls frolic toward the vineyards. Why do you not rise and walk with them?

Arise, my heart, arise and walk with the dawn, for night has passed. The terrors of the night have disappeared with its dark dreams.

Arise, my heart, and raise your voice in song, for only the children of darkness fail to join in the hymns of the morn.

A Lamentation
in the Field

At sunrise, just before the Sun emerged from behind the glow of dawn, I sat in the midst of the fields communing with nature. At that hour of purity and beauty, when man lies wrapped in the blankets of sleep—sometimes lost in dreams and at other times awake—I lay with my head upon the grass, asking all that I saw to explain the reality of beauty and asking all that was visible to tell me of the beauty of reality.

When I had distinguished my conceptions from those of other men, and had dispelled my illusions by freeing my spiritual self from matter, I became aware that my spirit had begun to grow and that something of nature had drawn nigh to me to teach me its deepest secrets and make me understand the language of its creatures.

While I was in this state, a breeze passed, sighing through the branches of the trees—the sigh of a despairing orphan. Seeking to understand, I asked, "Pleasant breeze, why do you sigh?"

It answered, "Because I go toward the City, driven by the warmth of the Sun, to the City where the contagions of diseases will ride upon my pristine skirts and the poisonous breaths of men will cling to me. This is why you see me sad."

Then I turned to the flowers and saw drops of dew falling as tears.

"Beautiful flowers," I asked, "why do you weep?"

One of them raised its graceful head and said, "We weep because Man will come, cut us off at our necks, carry us away to the City, and sell us like slaves, though we are free. When evening comes and we wither, he will throw us into the dirt. How could we not weep when the cruel hand of man shall take us away from the field, our home?"

After a moment, I heard the brook mourning like a bereaved mother.

"Sweet brook," I asked, "why do you mourn?"

"Because I go unwillingly toward the City," it answered, "where Man will spurn me. Instead of me he will drink the juice of the grape and use me to carry away his filth. How shall I not weep when soon my purity will become foul?"

Then I heard birds singing a mournful anthem telling of grief.

"Beautiful birds, why do you grieve?" I asked.

A sparrow perched near me on the tip of a branch and said, "Soon will the son of Adam come with a hellish instrument to slay us as a scythe mows down the corn. Each of us now bids the others farewell, for we none of us knows which will escape the fated doom. How shall we not grieve when death follows us wherever we go?"

The Sun rose from behind the mountain, crowning the tops of the trees with diadems of gold. I asked myself, "Why does Man destroy that which nature builds?"

Solitude and Isolation

Life is an isle in a sea of solitude and isolation.

Life is an isle whose stones are hopes, whose trees are dreams, whose flowers are loneliness, whose springs are thirst—in the midst of a sea of solitude and isolation.

Your life, my brother, is an isle, cut off from all other isles and climes. However often you set sail in ships and boats for other strands, however many fleets and armadas call at your shores, you, you are the isle, alone in its plains, solitary in its joys, distant in its yearnings, its mysteries and hidden secrets unknown.

I saw you, my brother, seated upon a hill of gold, rejoicing in your wealth, unrivaled in your riches, in every handful of nuggets finding a hidden thread tying men's thoughts to yours, binding their desires to

yours. I saw you become a great conqueror, dispatch-
ing victorious legions to level mighty fortresses, taking
possession of impregnable strongholds.

Yet, when I looked at you again, beyond the walls
of your treasuries, I saw a heart throbbing in isola-
tion, thirsting unto death in a cage fashioned from
gold and jewels but empty of water.

I saw you, my brother, seated upon a throne of
glory. Around you stood men singing songs to your
name, chanting your praises, recounting your bestow-
als, looking toward you as though you were a prophet
whose great spirit would exalt their spirits as they
circled about it among the stars and planets. You
looked down at them, your face exultant, strong,
masterful as though you were the spirit and they were
the body.

But when I looked again, I saw your soul in its
solitude standing beside your throne, in torment at
its exile and choking in its desolation. Then I saw it
stretch out its hand in all directions as though it were
beseeching the aid of unseen forms. I saw it look
above the heads of the people toward some distant
place, toward a place empty of everything save soli-
tude and isolation.

I saw you, my brother, smitten with the love of a
beautiful woman. I saw you anoint the crown of her

head with the liquid essence of your heart, fill her palms with kisses. As she looked at you, affection shone in her eyes, and her lips held the sweetness of motherhood. I said in my heart, "Love has destroyed this man's solitude and wiped away his isolation. He is once again linked to that universal and all-embracing spirit, to that spirit that draws to itself by love what was cut off from it by emptiness and oblivion."

But when I looked at you again, I saw that your infatuated heart enfolded a solitary heart that desired to anoint the woman's head with its secrets and could not. Beyond your soul melting with love, I saw another soul, lonely. It was like a mist that desired to be transformed into teardrops in your beloved's hands but could not.

လ

Your life, my brother, is a lonely dwelling, far from the dwellings of living things.

Your spiritual life is a dwelling far from the paths of those appearances and phenomena that men call by your name. If this dwelling is dark, you will not be able to illumine it with your relative's lamp. If it is empty, you will not be able to fill it with the good things of your neighbor. If it stands in a desert, you will not be able to move it to a garden planted by another. If it is raised upon a mountain peak, you will not be able to bring it down to a valley trodden by the feet another.

The life of the soul, my brother, is surrounded by solitude and isolation. Were it not for this solitude and that isolation, you would not be you, and I would not be me. Were it not for this solitude and isolation, I would imagine that I was speaking when I heard your voice, and when I saw your face, I would imagine myself looking into a mirror.

A Ship in the Mist

We had gathered in his lonely house above the Vale of Qadisha, on a night black with wind-driven snow. He told this story as he stirred the ashes in the hearth with the end of a stick.

෴

My friends, do you wish to know the secret of my grief? Shall I relate the tragedy that is reenacted in my heart every day and night? You have wearied of my unbroken silence. You are bored with my sighs and mutterings, and you say to each other, "If this man will not let us enter the temple of his agonies, how shall we enter the house of his friendship?" You are right, my friends, for without a portion of my pain, you can share nothing else with me. Listen, then, to my story. Listen, but have no pity, for pity is shown to the weak, and I am ever strong in my agony.

Since the dawn of my youth, I saw continually in my daydreams and in the dreams of sleep the apparition of a woman, wonderful in her form and dress. While alone at night, I saw her standing near my couch, and I heard her voice in the silence. Sometimes when my eyes were closed, I could feel the touch of her fingers on my brow. I would open my eyes and rise in alarm, listening with all my being to the whisper of nothingness.

I often said to myself, "Has my imagination led me into such peril that I have become lost in the mist? From the vapors of my dreams have I constructed a woman fair of face, sweet of voice, gentle of touch, to take the place of a woman of breath and clay? Is my mind so disordered that it has taken a mental shadow as a companion for me to love and befriend, to lean upon, a companion in whose nearness I can distance myself from all men? Shall I close my eyes and ears to every living form and voice, see only her form, hear only her voice? The madman in discontent with his solitude will devise a companion and wife from the spectres of his solitude."

You are sceptical when I utter the word "wife." But this is one of those experiences that we cannot reject as absurd, however much we may wish to, for in reality they have left an indelible mark on our souls.

That imaginary woman was indeed my wife. She shared in all my life's wishes and hopes, all its joys and desires. Each morning when I awoke, I saw her sitting on the cushions of my couch, looking at me with eyes full of childhood's purity and a mother's compassion. Whatever task I attempted, she would aid me in its accomplishment. Whenever I sat at a table, she sat opposite me, talking with me and sharing her opinions and thoughts. When evening came, she would approach me and say, "Come, let us go out this evening among the hills and valleys. We have tarried long enough indoors."

I would leave my work and take her hand. By the time we reached the countryside, it would be cloaked in the dark veil of evening, exuding the magic of stillness. We sat side by side on a high rock watching the distant twilight. Sometimes she pointed to the clouds scattering the last rays of the sun. Sometimes she had me listen to the warbling of a bird, as he sang a hymn of thanksgiving and peace before seeking the shelter of his branch until morn.

How often did she enter my chamber while I was preoccupied with restless apprehension! No sooner did my eye fall upon her than my restlessness was turned to calm, my anxiety to cordiality and friendship.

How often when I met people did my soul become a battlefield where warring legions rebelled against the loathsomeness in their souls. But as soon as I recognized her face amongst theirs, the storm raging within me changed to celestial melodies.

How often I sat down alone, my heart run through with a sword forged of life's hardships, the problems of existence links of a chain about my neck! Then I turned my face and saw her standing before me, gazing down upon me with eyes shining with brilliant light. The clouds dispersed, my heart rejoiced, and life appeared a paradise of joys and delights.

You ask me, my friends, "Were you happy in this strange and singular condition?" You ask, "How is a man in the vigor of his youth able to content himself with what summons him from illusion, from imagination and dream—indeed, from a sickness in the soul?"

I answer that the years I passed in this way were, in their beauty and happiness, in their pleasure and peace, the best part of my life. I tell you that my ethereal companion and I were a pure and ideal thought, dancing in the light of the sun and drifting on the surface of seas, scudding like the moon through the night skies and rejoicing in such songs as no ear has ever heard, standing before visions that no eye has seen. Life—all of life—we experienced in our spirits. We knew all of existence, we comprehended it utterly, and we exulted in it and felt the pain of its agonies. All that I knew with my spirit, she also knew, each day and night, until I reached my thirtieth year.

Would that I had never reached the age of thirty! Would that I had died a thousand and one times before I attained that year! In it the core of my life was destroyed and the blood of my heart was drained away. It has left me to face the days and nights as a blasted tree, bare and alone, whose branches do not dance to the songs of the air and among whose leaves and flowers no bird will ever weave its nest.

꙼

The storyteller was silent for a moment. He bent his head and closed his eyes. He let his arms drop onto the chair and seemed the embodiment of despair. We sat silent and expectant, waiting to hear the rest of his tale. Then his eyes opened and, with a voice breaking out from the depths of his wounded spirit, he said:

You remember, my friends, that twenty years ago the governor of Mount Lebanon sent me on a scientific mission to the city of Venice, giving me a letter to the mayor of that city, whom he had known in Constantinople.

I left Lebanon and took passage on an Italian ship. That was in April, when the spring winds played in the air and bent low over the waves of the sea, carving lovely and ever-changing forms in the white clouds that veiled the horizons. How can I describe to you the days and nights that I passed aboard that ship? The powers of speech that men possess reach no further than what their senses can apprehend. The spirit comprehends that which is beyond sensation and is too subtle to be apprehended. How then can I describe those days and nights to you with words?

The years that I passed with my ethereal companion were given voice by love and companionship and overflowed with calm and contentment. In my happiness I little knew what pain lay in wait for me or what bitter dregs lay in the depths of my cup. No, I never feared that the flower that had blossomed above the clouds would wilt or that the anthem sung by the brides of the dawn would die away. When I left these hills and valleys, my companion was sitting by me in the carriage that carried me to the strand. In the three days I spent in Beirut before my journey, my consort went wherever I went and stopped wherever I stopped. If I met a friend, I saw her smiling at him. Whatever place I visited, I felt her hand holding mine. When I sat in the evening on the balcony of my lodgings, listening to the sounds of the city, she shared in my meditation and our thoughts ran as one. Then a boat carried me out to the ship from the dock in Beirut. No sooner had I set foot on the deck of the ship than I sensed a change in the spaces of my soul. I felt a strong unseen hand gripping my arm, heard a deep voice whispering in my ear, "Come back! Come back from where you have gone. Go back down to the boat and return to the shore of your homeland, and do not journey upon the sea."

The ship set sail. I stood on its deck like a sparrow in the talons of a hawk as it circles in the sky. When evening at last hid the peaks of Lebanon behind the mists of the sea, I found myself standing alone at the bow of the ship. The girl in my dreams, the woman I loved with all my heart, the wife who had been the companion of my youth was gone. The sweet maiden whose face I had seen whenever I gazed at the sky and whose voice I always heard in the silence, whose hand I felt whenever I stretched out my hand before me— she was not upon the deck of the ship. For the first time, for the first time, I found myself standing alone before the night and the sea and the sky.

In such a state I wandered distracted, calling to my companion in my heart, staring at the ever-changing waves, hoping to see her face in the white foam.

By midnight the other passengers had gone to their beds and I alone remained, wandering wretched and troubled. I suddenly looked up and saw her standing in the mists a few paces away. My body trembled. I stretched out my hand to her, calling, "Why have you forsaken me? Why have you left me in my loneliness? Where have you gone? Where are you, my companion? Come to me, come to me. Never leave me again!"

She did not approach me, but stayed fixed in her place. Then her face was filled with a pain and a grief whose like I have never seen in all my life. In a voice small and faint she said, "I have come from the depths of the sea to look upon you for a single moment, and then I will return to the depths of the sea. Go to your cabin, lie down, and dream."

As she said these words, she dissolved into the mists and disappeared. I called to her with the persistence of a hungry child. I reached out my arms in every direction, but they closed on air heavy with the damp of the night.

I went to my cabin, the elements of my spirit swirling, crashing together, falling, and rising. Within that ship I was another ship, tossed on a sea of despair and doubt. To my astonishment no sooner did I drop my head upon the pillows of my bunk than I felt a heaviness in my eyes and a torpor in my limbs, and I slept deeply until morning. While I slept I had a dream. I saw my companion crucified upon a flowering apple tree. Blood dripped from her palms and her feet onto its two branches and trunk, splattered the grass below, and mingled with the fallen petals.

Night and day the ship sailed on through the surging seas while I walked its deck, scarcely knowing whether I was a man journeying to a distant city on a human errand or a ghost wandering in a space filled only with mist. I could not sense the nearness of my companion or see her face while awake or asleep. Fruitlessly I beseeched the hidden powers to let me hear the sound of her voice or glimpse her shadow or feel her fingertips upon my brow.

In such a condition I passed fourteen days. At noon on the fifteenth day, we saw the coast of Italy, and that evening the ship entered the harbor of Venice. People came out in brightly painted boats to carry the passengers and their belongings to the city.

Of course you know, my friends, that Venice is a city built on dozens of little islands. Canals are its streets, the houses and palaces are built over the water, and boats take the place of carriages.

When I had climbed down from the ship into a boat, the boatman asked me, "Sir, where do you wish to go?" When I mentioned the name of the mayor of the city, he looked at me with great respect and began to row.

As the boat carried me along, night fell, casting its cloak upon the city. Lights appeared in the windows of the palaces, churches, and public buildings, and their reflections twinkled and bobbed on the water. Like a poet's dream, Venice was wondrous to see, a place of fantasy enrapturing me. As the boat reached the first bend of the canal, I heard innumerable bells, their ponderous, gloomy, frightful tolling filling the air. Though I was spiritually distant, separated from all exterior reality by my stupor, the sinister bronze bells rent the tablet of my breast like nails.

The boat stopped alongside a flight of stone stairs rising from the water to a dock. The sailor gestured to me and pointed to a palace rising from the midst of a garden. "This is your destination," he said. I got out of the boat and went slowly up toward the house. The sailor followed me, carrying my bag on his shoulder. I reached the door of the house and paid him his fee and tipped him. When I knocked on the door of the house, it opened and I found myself before of a group of servants. Their heads were bowed and they were weeping and lamenting with choked voices. I was astonished at this sight and unsure of what I should do.

After a little while, a middle-aged servant approached me and looked at me with blood-shot eyes. In a sorrowful tone he asked, "What do you want, sir?"

I said, "Is this not the house of the mayor of the city?"

He nodded his head in confirmation.

With that I brought out the letter that the governor of Lebanon had given to me. Silently he looked at its address, then he walked slowly to a door in the back of the antechamber.

All this occurred without any thought or deliberation on my part. I went over to a young chambermaid and asked her the cause of their sadness and mourning. She answered sorrowfully, "Have you not heard that the daughter of the mayor died today?"

She said nothing more, but covered her face with her hand and gave herself up to weeping.

Consider, my friends, the condition of a man who had crossed the seas as if he were a confused, nebulous thought, giants of the air driving him to ruin among murky waves and ashen mists. Imagine the state of a young man who had traveled two weeks suspended between his cries of despair and the roaring of the sea. As soon as he reached his journey's end, he found himself standing at the door of a house within which stalked spectres of grief and whose corners were filled with cries of mourning. Imagine, my friends, a foreigner seeking the hospitality of a house overspread with the wings of death.

The servant who had carried my letter to his master returned. Bowing he said, "Welcome, sir. The mayor is expecting you."

With that he led me to a door at the end of the corridor. He motioned for me to enter. I found myself in a large, high-ceilinged room lit by candles. A number of notables and priests were sitting there, all enveloped in profound silence. I had gone only a few steps when an old man with a white beard rose in the middle of the room. Cares had bent his back, and pain had plowed furrows in his brow. He approached me, took my hand, and said, "You honor us by coming from a distant land, yet you find us bereft of that which was dearest to us. Still I hope that our affliction will not hinder the errand for which you came. You need not be concerned, my son."

I thanked him for his kindness and said a few confused words of consolation for his grief.

The old man led me to a chair next to his seat. I sat silent among the other silent people, glancing furtively at their melancholy faces and listening to their sighs. A lump of pain and anxiety formed in my heart. After an hour the people began to leave, one by one, until only I was left in that mute room with the unhappy father. Then I too stood up, turned to him, and said, "Sir, permit me to depart."

But he would not allow this, and replied, "No, my friend, do not go. Be our guest, if you are able to tolerate our grief and our sighs of mourning."

His words abashed me, and I bowed my head in acquiescence. Then he spoke to me again, saying, "You Lebanese revere the guest more than any other people. Why not remain with us so that we can show you some small part of what the stranger receives in your land."

After a moment the unfortunate old man rang a silver bell, and there entered a chamberlain in a livery embroidered with silver and gold. The old man gestured toward me and said, "Take our guest to the east room and see that he has food and drink. Attend personally to his needs and sit watchful while he rests."

The chamberlain led me to a spacious room, handsomely designed and richly appointed. Paintings and silk hangings covered its walls. In the center was a fine bed covered with blankets and brocade pillows.

The chamberlain left me alone. I slumped into a chair, thinking of myself and my surroundings, of my exile and my loneliness, of the events of my first hour in this place far from my land.

The chamberlain returned and set a tray of food and drink before me. I ate a little but without appetite, then I dismissed the chamberlain.

Two hours passed. I walked about the room or stood staring out the window at the sky, listening to the voices of the boatmen and the rhythmic splashes of their oars. Exhausted by the late hour and my morbid thoughts about life and its mysteries, I finally threw myself onto the bed, seeking the consolation of an oblivion that harmonizes the stupor of sleep and the consciousness of wakefulness, that alternates memory and forgetting like the rhythm of the sea as it rises and falls. I was like a soundless battlefield on which silent armies fought; death struck down their horsemen and the silent men died.

No, my friends, I do not know how many hours I spent in that state. There are courtyards in life through which our spirits pass, but we cannot measure their dimensions by such human contrivances as time and distance.

No, I do not know how many hours I remained in that state. All that I knew then—all that I know now—is that while I was in that confused state I was aware of a living presence standing near my bed, aware of a power trembling in the air of the room, aware of an ethereal being calling out to me without a voice, startling me without a motion. I rose to my feet and went out into the antechamber—driven, commanded, drawn by an overpowering compulsion. I went, but not by my will. I went like a sleepwalker. I went in a world beyond all that we reckon as time and space. When I reached the end of the antechamber, I entered a large room in the midst of which was a bier surrounded by flowers and lit by two candles shining like stars. I approached it and bowed to look. I looked—and saw the face of my companion. I saw the face of the companion of my dreams behind the veil of death. I saw the woman whom I had loved with a love beyond love. I saw her, a stiff, white corpse in a white shroud amidst white flowers, overshadowed by the silence of the ages and eternity's terror.

My God, God of love and life and death, Thou it was who gave our spirits being then left them to journey among these lights and shadows. Thou it was who created our hearts and made them to throb with hope and pain. Thou, Thou who showed me my companion as a body grown cold. Thou it was who led me from one land to another to manifest to me the design of death in life, the will to pain in joy. Thou it was who made a white lily to grow in the deserts of my loneliness and solitude, then made me to travel to a distant valley to show it to me again—faded, withered, and dead!

Yes, my friends, friends in my desolation and exile, it was the will of God that gave me to drink of this cup of bitterness. Let the will of God be done! We are only mortal, only motes of dust swirling in an endless and unbounded void. Ours is only to submit and obey. If we love, our love neither comes from us nor belongs to us. If we are happy, our happiness is not in us but in life itself. If we feel pain, our pain is not in our wounds but in all of nature.

I do not tell you this story in complaint. The one who complains doubts life, and I am among the believers. I believe in the goodness of this gall that is mixed with every drop I drink from the cups of night. I believe in the beauty of these talons that rend my breast. I believe in the kindness of those steel fingers that tear at the fabric of my heart.

This is my story, but how shall I end that which has no end? I remained bowed before the bier of that girl whom I had loved in my dreams, staring at her face until the fingers of dawn touched the window glass. I stood and returned to my room, leaning upon the pains of man, bent beneath the burdens of eternity.

After three weeks I left Venice and returned to Lebanon, returning like one who had spent a thousand centuries in the depths of fate. I returned like every Lebanese returns—from exile to exile.

Forgive me, my friends, forgive me, for I have spoken too long!

The Unseeing Force

Spring came. As nature spoke with the tongues of brooks, hearts filled with delights. She smiled with the lips of flowers, giving joy to the soul. Then she angered and smashed the fair city, making man to forget the sweetness of her words and her gentle smiles. A blind power, terrifying, razes in an hour what generations had erected. The grasping fingers of unjust death encircle necks and crush them. A consuming power devours wealth and lives. Pitch-dark night hides the beauty of life beneath a blanket of ashes. Terrifying elements pour out from their places of ambush to slaughter helpless men, to make ruins of their houses, to scatter in haste what they gathered with patience. A violent earthquake, the labor pains of pregnant earth, gives birth in agony to naught but ruin and misery.

As this happens the sorrowing soul looks on from afar in reflection and pain. She reflects on the power of man to resist the irrational forces. She suffers with the afflicted as they flee fire and ruin. She reflects on the enemies of the Son of Man hidden beneath the surface of the earth and among the atoms of the æther. She suffers with the bereaved mothers and hungry babes. She reflects on the cruelty of matter and its contempt for precious life. She suffers with those who yesterday laid down to sleep in the shelter of their homes yet today stand far away, mourning their fair city with agonized sobs and bitter tears. She reflects on how hope is transformed into despair, joy into sorrow, ease into torment. She suffers with the hearts trembling in the talons of despair, sorrow, and pain.

Thus the soul stood in reflection and pain, sometimes led to doubt the justice of the laws binding the forces to each other. Sometimes she once again whispers into the ears of silence, "Beyond all beings there is an eternal wisdom, fashioning from such disasters and misfortunes a good whose results we do not see. The fire, earthquakes, and storms are, in earth's body, like the hatred, malice, and evil in the human heart. They rage and clamor—and abate. From their rage and clamor and from their abating the gods create the profound knowledge that man acquires at the price of his tears and blood and treasure."

Memory fixed me in my place. The misfortune of this nation fills the ears with moans and wailing. Before my eyes the forms rose up of all the trials and misfortunes that had taken place in the theatre of bygone days. In every century I saw man raise up towers and castles and temples upon the breast of the earth and I saw earth take them back into its heart. I saw the powerful rearing mighty buildings. I saw the mason shaping stones into statues and friezes, artists decorating walls and vestibules with pictures and tapestries. Then I saw this dry earth open its mouth and gulp down all that skilled hands and keen minds had gathered, cruelly defacing those statues and friezes, destroying in its wrath those drawings and carvings, burying in its violence those stately pillars and walls, acting the part of a beautiful woman, with no need of the devices fashioned by the Son of Man, contenting itself with the green meadow's raiment embroidered with the gold of the sands and the pebbles as jewels.

Amidst these terrifying disasters and horrible and debilitating afflictions, I found man standing like a giant mocking the stupidity of the earth and the wrath of the elements. Standing like a pillar among the ruins of Babylon and Nineveh, of Palmyra and Bombay and San Francisco, he sang an anthem of immortality, "Let the earth take back its treasure, for I am infinite!"

Before the Throne of Beauty

I escaped from society and wandered in the broad valley, sometimes following the course of a brook and sometimes listening to the conversation of the sparrows. At last I reached a place sheltered by branches from the eye of the Sun. I sat there conversing in solitude, communing with my soul. A thirsty soul sees all that is seen in mirages and all that is not seen in drink.

When my mind broke free from the cage of matter to soar in the heaven of imagination, it beheld a girl standing not far from me, a houri with no jewelry or raiment save a grape vine with which she concealed part of her figure. A diadem of anemones bound her golden hair. When she realized from my stares that I was transfixed by surprise and astonishment, she said, "I am the daughter of the forests, so do not fear."

I replied, though the sweetness of her voice had taken away my breath, "Does someone like you inhabit this land of desolation and wild beasts? Tell me who you are and whence you come."

She sat on the grass and said, "I am the symbol of nature. I am the virgin whom your fathers worshipped, building altars to her in Baalbek, Aphek, and Byblos."

I answered, "Those temples are fallen in ruins, and the bones of my ancestors are scattered upon the face of the earth. No trace remains of their gods or their religions save a few leaves buried in books."

She replied, "Some gods live only so long as their worshippers live and die with their deaths. Some live in divinity from the beginning that had no beginning until all eternity. But my beauty is dependent on the beauty you see wherever you turn your eyes. Beauty is nature in its entirety. Beauty is the beginning of the happiness of the shepherd among the hills, of the villager in the fields, of the tribes wandering between mountain and desert. For the wise man, beauty is the stairway to the throne of a reality that does not wound."

I spoke, but the pounding of my heart said what the tongue did not know, "Beauty is a terrifying and awful power."

The smell of flowers was upon her lips and the mysteries of life were in her eyes. "You men fear all things, even yourselves. You fear the sky, though it is the fountainhead of security. You fear nature, though it is the couch of repose. You fear the Great God, and ascribe to him malice and anger, though if He is not love and mercy, He is nothing!"

After a silence mingled with gentle dreams, I asked, "What is this beauty? Men differ in their definitions and knowledge of it just as they differ in how they praise and love it."

"It is what you are drawn to by your own soul. When you see it, you desire to give, not to receive. When you encounter it with hands outstretched from the depths of your soul, you draw it into those depths. Bodies reckon it affliction, but souls reckon it grace. It is the union of sorrow and joy. It is what you see though it is veiled, what you know though it is unknown, what you hear though it is silent. It is a power rising in the Holy of Holies of your essence and ending beyond your imaginations. . . "

The daughter of the forests drew close to me and laid her perfumed hand upon my eyes. When I opened them, I found myself alone in that valley. As I went home, my soul chanted, "When you see beauty, you desire to give, not to receive."